For Caregivers,
with Love

For Caregivers, with Love

GRETA REY

Baker Books

A Division of Baker Book House Co
Grand Rapids, Michigan 49516

Published by Baker Books
a division of Baker Book House Company
P.O. Box 6287, Grand Rapids, MI 49516-6287

Printed in the United States of America

Library of Congress Cataloging-in-Publication Data

Rey, Greta, 1936–
    For caregivers, with love / Greta Rey.
      p. cm.
    ISBN 0-8010-5705-1 (pbk.)
      1. Caregivers—Prayer-books and devotions—English. 2. Caring—
Religious aspects—Christianity. I. Title.
BV4910.9.R48   1996
242'.66—dc20   95-42627

To Betty De Vries
Caring Friend
Mentor
Colleague
Encourager
Who has made many things possible
For whom I thank God

Contents

7

Contents

Contents

Acknowledgments

Special thanks to
Doris Rey—sister, best friend, supporter, encourager, much more—for your invaluable love, help, and criticism that made this book possible
Gertrude Broekema Rey—mother who started it all—for your loving encouragement
Aline Leep Talsma—friend, mind stretcher, soul stretcher, who often has kept me afloat in troubled waters—for your reading and essential helpful insights
Donna Pastoor Penning—cousin-friend, frequent caregiving companion—for your unfailing cheerfulness, dependability, and loving patience
Laurel Hazel—friend, always a refuge in stormy times—for your love and understanding
Don De Young—most caring pastor, most careful preacher—for your prayers and affirmation of my thoughts
Beth Olson, Dorothy and Earl Stonerock—neighbors—for letting me use your stories

Introduction

My term as a caregiver of various relatives consumed the better part of a decade, was sporadic before that, and is not yet over. It was never easy and not always pleasant, a roller-coaster existence that exacted from me an emotional, spiritual, physical, financial, and professional toll.

I believe that I in some measure have had a full range of caregivers' emotions. In each instance I did what I thought was right or the only thing possible. However, looking back, I see that many of the unhappy experiences resulted from my ignorance, lack of resolve, wrong thinking, and unwise choices.

The valuable things I learned along the way, however, are countless, my spiritual development considerable, the richness of love from friends and supporters immeasurable, and my mother's and sister's inner beauties, which emerged for me to see, incomparable.

Most caregivers do not break. I did. At that point I found the simplest basic prayer for my needs— for peace, strength, and wisdom. With help I gained restoration of my health; with time and experience I gained cherished insights.

Knowing what I know now, would I do it again? Certainly, although not in all the same ways. But I would expect the same outcome: to know intensely God's love of me and my cared-for loved ones.

Introduction

My prayer for strength, peace, and wisdom has remained my constant and basic request of God for my life. It is also my prayer for other people, for it covers every other need. Therefore, I have used its three words to title each section of these writings for caregivers. I have also included the three texts from the Bible that I have clung to over the years.

Now I can encourage caregivers in whatever their situations, whoever their cared-for persons. Human love is our most intense and accurate aspect of ourselves as having been created in God's image; human compassion is our most intense and accurate aspect of ourselves as followers of Jesus. But human love can waver, and human compassion can weaken, and from time to time we caregivers need the encouragement that can best come from others who "have been there."

This is not a how-to book, not an instructional or informational handbook for caregiving. That type of material is readily available in most communities. Rather, its intent is to encourage the millions of nonprofessional persons who care for relatives, friends, and acquaintances, persons who need recognition and emotional and spiritual support. But, of course, professional or paid caregivers' work and personal involvements with their clients—and therefore their emotional and spiritual needs—largely overlap and parallel those of the nonprofessionals.

I pray for all caregivers and those they care for that God will give them peace, strength, and wisdom. They will rejoice when they recognize and accept God's answer to that prayer.

We Are the Caregivers

We care for
parents
children
spouses
siblings
friends
neighbors
males
females
young
adults
elderly

We care for
ill
infirm
disabled
underabled
recovering
slipping
overstressed
underblessed

15

For Caregivers, with Love

We care in
    our homes
    their homes
    single homes
    communal homes
    rich homes
    poor homes
    uptown
    downtown
    small towns
    no towns
    hometowns
    out-of-town

We care
    full time
    part time
    short times
    long times
    sometimes
    anytime
    overtime
    odd times

We are
    married
    single
    male
    female
    unemployed
    employed
    poor
    rich
    weak
    strong

We Are the Caregivers

young
old
experienced
learning
wondering
sure
reluctant
eager
poor in spirit
jubilant
in need
blessed
discouraged
encouraged

We are the caregivers.
We are a multitude.

PART

One

STRENGTH

Cast your burden on the LORD,
And He shall sustain you. . . .
—Psalm 55:22 NKJV

Cast all your anxiety on him
because he cares for you.
—1 Peter 5:7

1

Caregiver's Prayer for Strength

God,
The complexities and demands of this caregiving task take enormous strength. You know the physical strength I need to do my work; you know the emotional strength I need to remain steadfast; you know the spiritual strength I need to have hope and not despair.

You are my source of all the kinds of special strength I need. Show me your strength as you support me in the large things; assure me of your strength as you encourage me in the small things.

2

Same Old Things

Another day.
Same old things.

Why is it that body functions
When they function
Are subjects infrequently discussed,
Fall into such insignificance
They become life's oversights?

I'll get up
In a few minutes.

But when body functions
Fail to function
They take on
Major proportions,
Major importance,
Major time consumption,
Main subjects of conversation;
Move to the forefront
Of life's efforts—

21

Strength

Focused hurdles,
Fair accomplishments.

Yes,
I heard you.

Father in heaven,
Did you ever think that
You got things topsy-turvy?
All this time and
Energy and
Money and
Conversation and
Concentration
On body functions
That don't function?
This was your intention?

Okay.
Give me time.

Bed
Bathroom
Breakfast
Pills
Medicine
Dressed
Moved
Comfortable

Uh, huh,
Be patient.

Clean his face
Clean his hair
Clean his teeth

Same Old Things

Clean his messes
Clean his body
Clean his odors

Clean his bed
Clean his clothes
Clean his room
Clean his equipment

Clean the bathroom
Clean the kitchen
Clean the sitting room
Clean the rest. . . .

I'm
Getting up.

Why is it that soul functions
When they function
Are subjects infrequently discussed,
Fall into such insignificance
They become life's oversights?

Don't worry,
I'm coming.

And that soul functions
When they malfunction
Are also subjects infrequently discussed,
Fail to be acknowledged,
Fall victim to oversight?

I'll be
Right there.

Strength

Body and soul
Go together.
Soul functions
Are love
Giving and getting—
Soul to soul
Together
Contemplating
Concentrating
Connecting
Consummating
Through body functions.

I'm
Up now.

Body and soul
Go together.
Inside his malfunctioning body
Is his precious soul
That needs
Loving
Giving and getting,
Connecting with mine
Through
His malfunctioning
Body functions.

I'm on
My way.

Father in heaven,
Did you ever think that
I would think that
Topsy-turvy could be
Right side up?

Same Old Things

Ahh,
All my parts
Are functioning!

Thank you, God.

Here I am.
Good morning, dear one.

3

God Is

God is God
not because of
not identified with
not defined by
not synonymous with

But
in spite of
inside of
outside of

what happens.

And no matter
what happens
what doesn't happen
what I do
what I don't do
what God does
what God doesn't do,

God Is

God is love.

God loves
you.
God loves
me.

God's love
is
God's glory.

4

Caregiver's Communications

*L*ord,
remind me not to run off at the mouth
and bore everyone with my problems.
Open my eyes to the life beyond my life
and to the people with lives outside my walls
so I can give them the courtesy of listening to
    them
and consider their need for two-way
    friendship.

On the other hand, Lord,
remind me not to be so protective of other
    people's
time and tolerance and interest in their own
    life situations
that I so belittle my own situation

28

Caregiver's Communications

I never give myself the courtesy of saying,
  "Yes, this is how it is,"
  nor consider my own human need to
    communicate.

Lord,
One of your supreme gifts to me
is my friend the listener
who lets me talk until I'm talked out,
who never says, "You already told me that,"
when I have—a thousand times—
who never demands equal time,
and who after the talk is over
gives me the courtesy of sharing normal
    activities outside my walls
but considers my need to set the agenda.

5

Caregiver's Connections

Lord,
Remove my blinders
when my cared-for person has become
the most concentrated object of my narrow
focus,
or I have concentrated my narrow focus on
myself as caregiver.

Lord,
Spread out my myopic view that
my cared-for person has only one
caregiver—me;
for scarcely any cared-for person has only
one caregiver,
and both are connected to shared-time and
secondary caregivers:

spouses, children, siblings, parents,
relatives, friends, neighbors
who care directly for the cared-for person
or who care indirectly by caring for the
caregiver;
we both are connected to tertiary caregivers
who likely are overlooked and
do not think of themselves as caregivers:
supporters who drive for us or sit in for us
or shop for us,
workmates who cover for us and pick up
the extra work when we must be away
tending our cared-for persons or ourselves,
neighbors who mind our children or feed
our pets or watch our houses,
acquaintances who send notes or cards or
flowers or meals,
pastors who call on us and remind us of
your comforts;
and we are connected to
Christians who pray for us and
kind nurses at the other end of the phone
who reassure us and
friendly clerks who accept our endlessly
returned purchases and
unquestioning appointment schedulers
who make our changes
and on and on.

6

Caregiver's Community

*L*ord,
How far does this caring community extend?
When you show me who lives beyond the
   walls of my existence
and you show me whom you have circulated
   inside my walls
I no longer see the walls
but see that you have made me and my
   cared-for person
part of your kingdom that has no end—
your kingdom of love.

These tears are tears of gratitude.

And now excuse me, please; I have thank-you
   notes to write,
dishes to return, phone calls to make.

7

Trying Times

Trial
Temptation
Test—
  Synonyms.
  I looked them up.

My significant synonym?
I know, Lord,
I don't have to look it up:
Worry.

My worries?
You know, Lord,
Even when I don't look up.
  You know.

8

Now

God,
Make me assertive
In my resolve
To stay one step ahead of crisis
Instead of two steps behind
Striving to catch up.

Make me determined
To do what must be done
  When you have given me the wisdom
  To be objective and
  To know what's best for all concerned
  Even though it gives me the appearance
  Of hardheartedness.

Make me courageous
To stick to my decision and
Not give in to
  My cared-for one's physical condition
  Today (as though it would stay
  In the status quo)
  Or emotions

Or preferences
Or hope against hope
Or comfort of doing nothing
Except "just wait and see"—
And not give in to my own.

Make me strong
To resist my inclinations to
    Be the nice guy
    Or take the easy way out
    Or put it off
    Or not stir up the waters
    Or go along.

God,
Make me aware
Of the subtle snares
That paralyze our present
And bind our future.

9

It's Catching

I caught myself being foolish
Unintentionally,
Inadvertently, of course,
Out of the goodness
Of my heart.

I caught myself being too nice,
Dutifully,
Deferentially, that is,
Within the mindset
Of my caring role.

I caught myself being used
Unproductively,
Wastefully, in fact,
Because of the generosity
Of my nature.

I caught myself giving in
Lovingly,
Compassionately, I thought,
To the demands
Of my cared-for one.

It's Catching

I caught myself being drawn
Subtly,
Unwittingly, even,
Into my cared-for one's
Condition-based
Anxious illogic.

I caught myself being eroded
Attitudinally,
Then spiritually
By silent resentment
Toward my cared-for one.

I caught myself allowing
My cared-for one
To become
Self-absorbed,
Self-serving,
Spoiled.

I caught myself reading,
"If someone is caught
In a sin,
You who are spiritual
Should restore him gently. . . .
Carry each other's burdens."*

I caught myself thinking
Enlighteningly,
Circularly,
That both of us need
Considerable attention.

---

*Galatians 6:1–2a

Strength

I caught myself envisioning
Realistically
Restoring
Our reciprocal balance
Of mutual love.

I caught myself resolving
Firmly
Not to stay caught
In the self-centered focus
Of my cared-for one.

I must catch the courage
Tactfully,
Gently
To turn the attention
Of my cared-for one
From insatiable self-need
To my legitimate need
For considerate love.

God, I need to catch
Your restorative power.

10

Royal Power

The king was meeting with his council.

Said the money broker to the king, "You could be the wealthiest person in the world. You are the king! Use your brain power to your advantage. You have the national treasury at your disposal. Devise ways to make your subjects pay higher taxes, to feed and clothe and house you in high style. You never need to be hungry or uncomfortable. Live as luxuriously as you please. Shop! The world is your marketplace. And use your money to earn more money. Wealth increases wealth.

"You are the luckiest person in the world."

Said the king to the money broker, "I am the king. I am the provider. My responsibility is to make it possible for my citizens to feed and clothe and house themselves. My responsibility is to provide them with a healthy and comfortable environment. My responsibility is to be a model of helpfulness. I get my life from my citizens. We need each other.

"I am the king."

Said the power broker to the king, "You could be the most powerful person in the world. You are the

king! Use the power of your position to your advantage. You have the military forces at your command. You can force your subjects to do for you
whatever you want. Make them protect you, fight
your battles, eliminate all your enemies, conquer
the world. You need never fear anyone or anything.
Now, what could be more satisfying—more fun—
than to order the rest of the world around? Power
builds power.

"You are the luckiest person in the world."

Said the king to the power broker, "I am the king.
I am the protector. My duty is to work for my
citizens, to look out for their best interests, to
strengthen them. Life is grubby. If I don't get into
it with them, how can I know how to help them
cope with life or to lead them to a better way? My
duty is to aid them in building their community and
then to support it. I give my citizens their security.
I live my life with my citizens. We trust each other.

"I am the king."

Said the public-relations broker to the king, "You
could be the most famous person in the world. You
are the king! Use the power of your charisma to
your advantage. You have the communications
media wrapped around your little finger. You can
make yourself as popular with your subjects as you
want. You can persuade them to honor you and to
advertise to the rest of the world how wonderful
and amazing you are. What could make you feel
more exhilarated than to have everyone's recognition and adulation? Fame spreads fame.

"You are the luckiest person in the world."

Said the king to the public-relations broker, "I am
the king. I am the enhancer. My privilege is to honor
my citizens, for I value every one of them, and I

want them to see they are all worthwhile to each other. I comfort them and give them hope. I raise their sights for now and for the future. My privilege is to pay close attention to them and to assure their happiness. I want my citizens to feel privileged to belong to this kingdom. I devote my life to my citizens. We love each other.

"I am the king."

The ego builder exploded in exasperation. "What are you talking about? You are the **king**! I don't get it. You can have what most people only wish for, more of what anyone else has. Wealth! Power! Fame! You can have whatever you want!

"Yet you . . . you . . ."

"Yes," the king said proudly, "I can be fulfilled, effective, appreciated, for I have the highest calling in the world.

"*I am a caregiver.*"

With that he coolly and permanently dismissed the council, appointed twelve new council members, sent for his donkey, and rode carefully through his kingdom.*

---

*Read Matthew 4:1–11. Then read the rest of the four Gospels.

11

More of That Fruit

Well-meaning people
Well-researched Bibles
Well-deliberated interpretations
Well-delivered sermons
Well-phrased theologies
Well-spoken responses
Well-tested hypotheses
Well-developed theories
Well-documented treatises
Well-reasoned philosophies
Well-placed positions
Well-aimed answers
    To the question,
      Why?

Well!
    Then there was
      I
Grasping all the answers
Of the well-meaning people

Who cultivate their answers
  So they can
    Edify.

   I,
Who deeply craved the answers
  To the question,
    Why?
Voraciously swallowed
All the well-aimed answers
From the well-meaning people
Whether they satisfied
    Or not.

Now what have I got?
  Consternation due to
  Contradiction.

   I
Don't feel well.

Lord,
In my quest for control
Over what we endure
I was tempted to find
You accountable and
Allowed myself to be lured
Into answer overindulgence.

Now, please,
Administer the cure
And purge me of
  The question,
    Why?

12

To Do Is To Be

Some people are meant to be caregivers.
   I am one.
   Thank you for giving me this aptitude for
giving care
     now that I need it.

Some people are not meant to be caregivers.
   I am one.
   Thank you for giving me this courage to
give care
     now that I need it.

13

Special People

God,
This is a special prayer
For special strength
For special people—
Other caregivers.

"Togetherness;
Strength in numbers;
Mutual concern;
Not alone;
Not the only one;
Part of a group;
Misery loves company;
Share;
To know others. . . ."

If caregivers know
Another caregiver—
Someone who understands—
Is praying for them,
They get more strength
From the prayer
And because of the prayer.

Strength

If I do not see or meet
The other caregivers,
You do.
If they do not read this,
You do.

Whether or not they know it,
You do know
This prayer
For strength for caregivers,
    For you are always
    The special one
    In our group
    Of special people.

14

Confession

Some people don't care, and it
Makes
Me
Mad.

Never mind how others suffer or have needs
they can't meet by themselves.

They won't help.

Never mind that someone else carries the
load of tending the afflicted.

They won't do their part.

No, they let other people do all the work,
while they go on their merry ways.

How can they be so blind, so unfeeling?

Oh, they are busy, all right,
busier than the rest of us—

attending their kids' ball games, maintaining
  their houses and yards,
playing in their sports leagues, keeping up
  their healthy good looks,
going on shopping sprees, planning another
  vacation, not missing a movie or a thing on
  TV,
getting bogged down when their mechanical
  and electronic toys don't work,
knowing the fates are ganging up against
  them when they miss a beat for removal of
  an ingrown toenail.
They even do church activities.

Where is their sense of duty? responsibility?

To top it all, they are so happy, so energetic,
so unburdened, so unfrazzled, so . . .
  disgusting!

Oh, God, I do envy them!

But
What do I know
About
Them?

15

They Never Visit

It requires a certain kind of strength
And a certain measure of grace
Or courage or determination
Or shove from sense of duty
For many people to enter the environment
Of the cared-for person
To visit.

I sympathize
With those who know they do not have
Or do not believe they have
What it takes
To be a good visitor.

I sympathize
With those who are frightened
By what they know they will encounter
Or by the unknown
Or by its possible effect on them
And how they will act or react.

Strength

But there may be
Another reason why
"They never visit"—
They have no reserves
Of strength or grace
Or courage or determination
To return to the scene
And encounter memories of past griefs
Over sufferings
Or unbearable conditions
Or unresolved issues
That surrounded other cared-for persons.

I sympathize,
For I'm not sure
I will be able
To return
To the scene.

16

Power Surge

Prayer is a power surge.

Prayer is the connecting instant
  When you suddenly touch God,
  And God touches you.

Prayer is the connecting instant
  When you consciously reach
  Or are reached unawares.

Prayer is the connecting instant
  When spirits human and divine
  Leap a chasm and bond.

Prayer is the connecting instant
  When hope becomes energy
  And God's promise empowers.

Prayer is the connecting instant
  When God's power becomes
  Your life strength.

Prayer is God's power surge.

17

Crisis!

It's time for you to kick in, God,
And take full responsibility.

Responsibility.
That's what I've been taking
All this time,
Of course.
Since my cared-for one first needed me
I've never questioned
My responsibility.

Responsibility; response; must respond to.
To what?
Whatever I see needs doing—
And do it;
Whatever needs taking care of—
And take care of it;
Whatever needs bearing—
And bear it;
Whatever is wrong—
And make it right.

If I can.

Crisis!

But now I can't.

Everyone has dreaded this crisis.
My cared-for one dreaded this crisis.
But I dreaded it most.
I did everything I could to prevent it.
I hoped against hope it would stay away.
I told myself it would not necessarily take
   place.
I said it was the worst-case scenario and very
   unlikely to play out.
I believed God would not have us suffer
   much more than we already have.
I was sure God loved us too much to let this
   happen.

I worked.
I planned.
I hoped.
I prayed.
And prayed still more.

I believed.
Yes, I came to believe
I need not worry about this crisis.

I went on with my responsibility
And into partnership with God.
It was a good partnership.
God and I worked together for my cared-for
   one.
God gave me strength.
God snapped the situation into better
   perspective for me.

Strength

God drew me back from my cared-for one's
    suffering.
God helped me be more objective.
God salved my incredulity and anger.
God sustained my cared-for one
Night and day.

I worked.
I planned.
I hoped.
I prayed.
I believed.

Still I dreaded.

Now the very crisis
Everyone dreaded
Is here.

I can no longer prevent it.
My hope is history.
I do not see the necessity of this crisis;
It serves no purpose, helps no one, will
    change no one for the better.
I see that the worst possible is reality.
I believe God wants us to suffer, and
I cease to speculate how bad the suffering
    still can get.
God's love for us right now?
Well, I confess I have little twinges of
    imagination of God's hate.

God, do you hate us?
Why?

Crisis!

Yes, I worked.
I planned.
I hoped.
I prayed.
I believed.
Oh, how I exercised
All my responsibility
To prevent this crisis!

But now
It's your responsibility, God.
Your responsibility overrides mine;
This crisis has come about anyway.
Any bit of responsibility I retained
Is out of my hands
And in yours.

Up to a point we were partners, God.
Now we are beyond that point—
We have a crisis.
In crisis we are no longer partners,
And I am the partner who is left outside.
You have taken over
With a new team.
Do what you will with my cared-for one, God.

I will be outside in the waiting room
Waiting with your love
For your love.

18

How're Ya Doin'?

They seem to care, to understand,
But what do they mean when they say,
"Hi, how're ya doin'?" or,
"Ooh, how *are* you?"

Perhaps they mean,
Are you bearing up,
Are you able to do your duties,
Are you still strong and healthy;
Or is the stress getting you down?

Perhaps they want
To know that I'm doing just great
To reassure themselves that
If I can manage a tough situation
They could, too;
Bad isn't really bad.

Perhaps they want
To know that I'm not doing too well
To reassure themselves that
Situations can get unmanageable

How're Ya Doin'?

According to their worst imaginations;
Bad is really bad.

Perhaps they are being polite
And don't think much
About the question
Or care much
About the answer.

"Fine."

But a few—very few—
Ever mean,
Because a few—only few—
Ever guess,
That how I'm doing
Has everything
To do with
The level of
My cared-for person's
Well-being—
Or maybe nothing
To do with it.

God, help me to be patient
And understanding
If they are not mature
In their experience
Or understanding.

  Besides,
  How would
  I feel
  If no one
  Ever asked?

19

Spreadsheet

Love God
Love others
Love myself

Keep me balanced, Lord.

Love others
Love myself
Love God

Keep me balanced, Lord.

Love myself
Love God
Love others

Keep me balanced, Lord.

20

Role Reversal

God, in your care for me you gave me my sister.

> When I was the primary caregiver
> I thought of myself and our cared-for
>   one
> As the center around which
> Everyone else,
> My sister especially,
> Would revolve—naturally;
> But when she did not exactly,
> I suffered what I should not:
>   The "she shoulds"
>   And blindness
>   To her feelings and needs
>   And—worse—to the care
>   She already gave.
>
> My sister the caregiver
> As caring and giving
> As I ever was—

Strength

Sharing the love
  the decisions
    the anguish
    the logistics
    the disruptions
    the joys
  For our cared-for one—
Remained in my eyes
The secondary caregiver
  Assuming the role of
    supporter
    encourager
    cheer giver
    cheerleader
    back-up
    backer,
  Which she was.

But nothing remains static.

Our cared-for one changed,
As did I,
And my sister became
The primary caregiver
  Of our cared-for one
  And of me,
  Which, I think,
  She always was.

God, your blessing to me is my sister; my joy is to appreciate her; my privilege is to thank you. Every caregiver needs a "sister" caregiver, as you know. When you have provided one, open the caregiver's eyes to that gift from you.

21

On Earth As in Heaven

*W*ill,
Desire,
Wish—
  Synonyms.
God,
Your will-desire-wish
For us
Is clear to me:
  That we deliberately,
  Compassionately,
  Care for the sick and needy,
  Relieve suffering,
  Regard all persons respectfully,
Live as Jesus did—
  Lovingly.

Strength

Will,
Choice,
Determination—
  Synonyms.
 God,
 Your will-choice-determination
 For us,
 It's clear to me,
   Is not yet done
   Perfectly,
 But it shall be—
   Heavenly.

 God,
 Your will
 Is my command.

22

Lull

Lord,
Let me lie here
A little while
Longer
And luxuriate
Under the layers
Of your love.

23

Blaagh!

This is a bad day
Because I'm in a bad way.

I'm so sick of this situation.
How long will it go on?
Will it keep on getting worse
Instead of better?

I don't know which is more discouraging—
The daily grind and boring parts
Or just seeing the whole situation
Deteriorate.
Will it ever turn around
And improve?

Patience and strength
Are the same for me today
Because I lack both.
I have so slowed myself
To my cared-for one's pace
That some days I think I do
More waiting than waiting on.

Blaagh!

Every day is the same.
I no longer try patiently
To wait to see how it all will turn out—
There's nothing to see.
I need encouragement
To wait it out
And to keep going.

I didn't ask for this, you know,
But I'm doing what I don't want to do
Anyway, any way,
Well, not the greatest way
Today.

God,
I apologize for this awful funk.
I'm not exactly blaming you, understand,
Just making sure you are aware
I depend on you
To keep me up when I'm up
And boost me up when I'm down,
Because you are more dependable than I
And . . .

What's that?
That small voice inside my head?
That hymn . . .

"Strength for today and
Bright hope for tomorrow,
Blessings all mine,
With ten thousand beside!
Great is thy faithfulness, Lord,
Unto me."

Thomas O. Chisholm

24

The Coming

Sooner or later
All things end—
   The good and the bad,
   The pleasant and unpleasant,
   Beautiful and ugly,
   Healthy and unhealthy,
   Lightweight and serious,
   Exalting and humbling,
   Enriching, impoverishing,
   Fast moving and slow,
   Short term and long—
Sooner or later
All things end.

It's one of the ways
New things begin.

25

Focus

The end is in sight.
The END is in sight—
The glorious
Glory-filled
Endless
End!

26

Amen!

Today we laughed,
Today we sang,
Today we danced
On lighter feet.

PART TWO

WISDOM

Seek the LORD while he may be found;
call on him while he is near.

—Isaiah 55:6

27

Caregiver's Prayer for Wisdom

God,
I am continually having to make decisions—small, immediate, daily decisions, as well as major, far-reaching decisions—regarding my cared-for one. For that I need wisdom: knowledge, understanding, sound reasoning, and good judgment.

Hold me to your goal for me: to do what is best, that is, what is most loving, for my cared-for one. And remind me to consider what is loving to myself also.

28

Not the Motive

Guilt—
The one concept
Popularly applied
To why I'm doing
What I'm doing
And why I'm doing
How I'm doing—
If people's perception,
Including the professionals',
Is that
I'm not doing
Too well.

Guilt
For what?
That I used to be
Less than loving
And will forever try
To make it up?
That I now am
Less than loving
But merely do
What I'm constrained to do?

Wisdom

That I always feel
I never do
As much as I should
For my cared-for one?

Guilt?
I cannot say
It does not play
A part in some
People's perceptions
Of what they are
Or why they are
Caregivers—
Even mine
Sometimes.

But
I don't believe
That I could be
Motivated
Mainly
Or propelled
Perpetually
To do what I do—
What must be done
For my cared-for one—
By guilt.

Guilt
As motivator
Cannot last
But soon becomes
A detractor,
Negative reactor,
That I renounce.

Not the Motive

For though
What I do
Brings boredom or stress,
Frustration or sadness,
I go on,
Not feeling guilt
For normal reactions,
Not feeling guilt
For not feeling guilty,
But acting
Out of love and concern
For my cared-for one.

Positively.

29

The Hidden

I heard the complaints
  I cannot wait
  I'm much worse today
  Are you really sure?
  No, do it this way
And thought they were dissatisfactions with
  me.

I heard the suggestions
  You're busy but
  I thought we should
  Before you go
  Maybe you would
And thought they were manipulations of me.

I heard the protestations
  I hate to ask you
  No, never mind
  You don't have to
  If you have time
And thought they were considerations of me.

The Hidden

I heard the apologies
   I'm so sorry
   That's okay
   You're too good to me
   I'm in your way
And thought they were protections of me.

I heard the evasions
   I didn't want to tell you
   It will go away
   I knew you were tired
   I can manage today
And thought they were rejections of me.

I saw the silences
   halfhearted smiles
   downcast eyes
   lightly dropped shoulders
   deep stifled sighs
And knew they were responses to me.

   God, grant me the grace
   To hear and perceive
   Guilt
   As my cared-for one's
   Hidden vulnerability.

30
Trio of Days

Wedding
Day of commencing living for caring

Anniversary
Day of continuing loving and giving

Funeral
Day of concluding life's loving caregiving

31

Can You Top This? (1)

Whenever we play
"Can You Top This?"
Someone else
Usually can.

I have one person to care for
Someone else has two.

I have laryngitis
She has strep throat.

I have a cough
He has pneumonia.

I have a toothache
She has migraines.

I have a back-muscle spasm
He has a ruptured disk.

Wisdom

I have a pacemaker
She has congestive heart failure.

I have diabetes
He has cancer.

I had one leg amputated
She had two.

However,

Her two amputated legs
Will not restore my one.

His cancer
Cannot reverse my diabetes.

Her heart problem
Does not eliminate mine.

His ruptured disk
Does not ease my back-muscle spasm.

Her migraines
Do not cure my toothache.

His pneumonia
Cannot stop my cough.

Her strep throat
Will not improve my voice.

And I still have
My person to care for.

Can You Top This? (1)

Someone else's
Worse condition than mine
Cannot make mine
Any better.

Only I can do that.

32

Can You Top This? (2)

Whenever someone plays
"Can You Top This?"
We usually can.

Someone else has one person to care for
I have two.

She has laryngitis
I have strep throat.

He has a cough
I have pneumonia.

She has a toothache
I have migraines.

He has a back-muscle spasm
I have a ruptured disk.

She has a pacemaker
I have congestive heart failure.

He has diabetes
I have cancer.

She had one leg amputated
I had two.

However,

My being worse off
Than someone else
Does not make me better off.

Comparisons
Neither enhance nor degrade
Eliminate nor restore
My condition
Nor anyone else's.

Why do people play
"Can You Top This?"

33

Listen!

Caregiver, you will learn to be
A patient
   Listener
To people
   Who
   Want to
      Unload their problems
      Onto you,
      Fix yours,
      Tell you what to do,
      Judge your experience by theirs,
      Brag about their successes
      Or their cared-for person's
      Or grab your sympathy,
      Relate the wisdom of the ages,
      Pass along
      Irrelevant information
      Or folk remedies
      Or quack medicines.

Caregiver, you will learn to be
A patient
   Listener

Listen!

To people
   Who
   Need to
   Talk to you.

Caregiver, you will learn
To stretch yourself to be
A patient
   Listener
   Who listens
   Caringly.

Caregiver, you will learn to be
A patient
   Listener
   Who
   Can filter out
     What is useless,
     Unfair,
     Harmful
   To you.

Caregiver, you will learn to be
A patient
   Listener
   Who
   Can retain from
The people
   Who
   Talk to you
     Their genuine concern
     Their valuable wisdom
     Their usable advice
   Because they
   Have listened
   To you.

Wisdom

Caregiver, you will learn to be
A patient
   Reader
Of writers
   Who
   Try to
   Persuade you to . . .

34

To a New Caregiver

If you never
dreamed of what you must do for an adult, or
what you must do for a child,
used the equipment,
heard the words you now must know,
dealt with the healthcare system or
any such system,
had much nerve,
observed a condition similar to your cared-
   for one's,
gave up more than you expected for someone
   else,
You will learn.

Do not expect
   that all caregiving is unpleasant,
   that caregiving is a breeze,
   other people to do your duties,

other people to fully understand your
   cared-for one's condition,
other people to fully comprehend your
   situation,
everyone close to you to have the same
   insights or perspectives as yours,
everyone to pull their own weight,
to change anyone,
to comprehend everything at once.
Most things improve with time.

Do expect
   many rewards in caregiving,
   good days,
   bad days,
   to be surprised by your own strength,
   help and encouragement from unexpected
      sources,
   to provide emotional support to your
      cared-for one,
   more of your life to revolve around your
      cared-for one than you'd like,
   to be angry,
   to be shocked,
   to be surprised by what other people
      expect of you,
   to be changed by the caregiving experience,
   the unexpected.
Your sorrows will be multiplied, your joys
   will be multiplied.

35

Moment Care

Inside the nursing home
They roam
Purposefully
Maintaining the remainders
Of their former
Purposeful
Selves.

Bit by bit
By byte or megabyte
In spurts or clusters
Their brains
Delete their information
Leaving ever-larger spaces
On their memory boards
Across which the remaining bits of
    information
Can no longer connect.

We who met them only recently
Can merely guess at their loved ones'
    agony
When they see
These cared-for persons'
Former selves
Disappearing inexorably,
Nor can we comprehend
Their deep despair
When they received
The final diagnosis of
THE DIS-EASE.

We can merely guess at their loved ones'
    agony
When they see
These cared-for persons
Exist as those selves
Who little resemble
Their former selves
And who seldom connect with
Their formerly filled-in spaces of
Memories, recognitions, people,
    places,
Feelings, reasonings, manners,
Words. . . .

A living person
Though partially deleted
Is nevertheless a self;
But because loved ones cannot
    suspend
Connections to the past
Nor replace its loss,
They grieve
Each time they see.

Moment Care

Inside the nursing home
They roam.

We do not see a loss to us
But the remaining bits
Scattered among the spaces—
Stages of selves who exist
In present moments
Only,

Each moment a self-contained lifetime

Of pain—
    Fruitlessly groping across the spaces
    To access a deleted familiar something;
    Wandering in search of the unsearchable;
    Trying to escape whatever is wrong,
    Not knowing what is wrong;
    Wanting to be doing,
    So compulsively just doing;
    Angrily resisting reality
    And those who must hold them to it;

Or neutrality—
    Staring, at rest;
    Sleeping, at best;

Or pleasure—
    Connecting smiling eyes to smiling eyes;
    Joining a group of cheerful people;
    Sharing a birthday cake;
    Caressing soft hair;
    Suddenly accessing a beloved parent
    Or childhood moment and
    Someone to tell about it;

Wisdom

Watching birds at a feeder outside a
  window;
    Hearing a story, comprehended or not;
    Twirling to imagined music,
    Or singing along with real music;
  Returning a hug—
  A real not perfunctory hug.

At any given moment
Every one of us becomes a caregiver
Charged with
Relieving pain, providing pleasure,
Whether the moment is connected
To all of life's other moments
Or stands alone and self-contained
As one moment of a lifetime on
A simple string of
Simple moment-lifetimes.

Inside the nursing home
We who care
Do not dismiss the roaming souls
To their empty spaces
Or painful places
But grasp their remaining bits of potential
  joy
To replace the sorrows of their moments—
    Humor them with a cheerful greeting;
    Smile into their eyes;
    Draw them into our embrace;
    Warm them at our family-party table;
    Cheer them with our fun;
    Engage their observation;
    Help them live the moment-lifetime
    Happily.

90

Moment Care

Then we, too, have lived
A successful moment-lifetime
To be stored
On our happy-memories boards.

Perhaps this is easier for us
Who need not suspend connections to the
    past.

But no person exists—
Within whatever size or quality the moment-
    lifetime—
Who has no space
To receive and respond to
Respect and
Love.

Each of us lives a lifetime which,
On the grid of paths connecting it
To all other lifetimes
That occupy the spaces of time,
Is but a moment
Surrounded by the spaces of the eternity
That is occupied by
God's
Respect
And love
For us.

36

Flip Side

I am a parent;
  I am a child
  Who does God's bidding
  And my cared-for one's.

I am a manager;
  I am an employee
  Who is responsible to God
  And for my cared-for one.

I am a caregiver;
  I am a patient
  Who needs God's care
  And people to care for me.

37

Firstborn

In the patriarchal societies of old
The wealth of land and possessions,
The preservation of the family name,
The authority of heading a large extended
    family and
The attendant power over many people,
The honor of being an elder in the
    community,
Were bequeathed upon the firstborn—

A large order delivered inside a tiny
    package
Thrust into a life of responsibility.

Thus it has been
    Throughout the ages
    Throughout the various societies
    Throughout the world
For the firstborn.

Wisdom

Cultures have mandated it,
Historians have documented it,
Psychologists have analyzed it,
Firstborns have just known it.

Monarchs, dictators, tyrants,
Landowners, business owners, professional
    persons,
Rich families, poor families,
Large Victorian families, nuclear middle-class
    families, single-parent families
Have had their unique demands but this in
    common:
    A firstborn—

    Their large order delivered inside a tiny
        package
    Thrust into a life of responsibility.

Firstborns may be responsible
    to help look after the younger children,
    to work to help support the family,
    to help put the younger children through
        school,
    to see that permanently dependent children
        are cared for when their parents are no
        longer able,
    to care for the parents in their old age,
    to bring pride and recognition to the
        family,
    to assure the parents someone will always
        love them,

    or
    to be caregivers.

Firstborn

We have seen firstborns—young children—
who
bear extra measures of
care, responsibility, concern for
younger siblings who are
    temporarily or chronically or terminally
      ill,
    intellectually or emotionally
      challenged,
    missing one or both parents.

We have seen such young firstborns who are
    quiet, sober, worried,
    serious beyond their years,
    overlooked, left out, put upon.

With wise and sensitive parents they learn
    valuable, laudable characteristics:
    Compassion,
    Service,
    Sacrifice,
    Family loyalty,
    Respect for persons,
    and—always—
    Responsibility.

With wise and sensitive parents they
    will not
    Think they are less important,
    Believe their feelings don't matter,
    Be told too often,
      "Share,
      Feel sorry for,
      Make it easier,
      Take care of."

But we on the outside have
   Looked over young firstborns' heads and
   Asked the parents, "How is the cared-for
     child?"
     Prayed public prayers for the cared-for
      child,
     Sent cards and gifts to the cared-for child.
      We have been
      Thoughtful of the cared-for one,
      Thoughtless of the firstborn.

The next time you encounter

   A large order inside a small package
   Thrust into a life of responsibility,

Acknowledge the child
   Not as an appendage or afterthought to a
     younger cared-for sibling,
   Not as a "good helper" or a "nice" older
     sibling,
But as a
   Unique
   Whole
   Worthwhile
   Lovable
   Feeling

   Person.

38

Keepers

I'm doing the best that I can.

Take it one day at a time.

She means well.

We did what we thought best at the time.

You have to overlook a lot of things.

I'm not perfect, but my heart is in the right place.

Little things mean a lot.

You'll never regret what you do for your loved one.

Do it now.

I'm not doing this for a reward.

Wisdom

A bird in the hand is worth two in the bush.

What you don't know *can* hurt you.

I'll be praying for you.

"And now these three remain: faith, hope and
   love.
But the greatest of these is love."*

Don't forget to laugh.

---

*1 Corinthians 13:13

39

Let's Face It

Abuse can happen
  to caregivers by their cared-for persons or
  to cared-for persons by their caregivers.

Abuse is against
  the vulnerable
  by the powerful,
  or against
  those who believe themselves to be
  vulnerable
  by those who imagine themselves to be
  powerful.

  Caregivers can be parties
  in either arrangement.
  Cared-for persons can be parties
  in either arrangement.

Abuse breaks down
   emotional health
   spiritual well-being
   physical safety
   respect for persons
   self-respect of the abused
   self-respect of the abuser.

Abuse relief begins
   when abusers
   or the abused
   acknowledge and face up to the abuse,
   seek God's help
   for deliverance from abuse,
   and seek out God's gift of human helpers
   of abused and abusers.

   To make that beginning
   is a caregiving responsibility,
   an act of love to the self
   and to the other.

Abuse is never
   inevitable
   necessary
   acceptable.

40

As We Also . . .

To give care
Many a caregiver
Must first forgive
The cared-for person's
Past.

To forgive
Is not to forget—
For that is impossible—
But to suspend
Remembered impediments to
Perfect respect.

While the past
May be prologue
It is not the present,
Where the need for care
Presides.

Wisdom

Conditional care
Cannot exist
When survival or healing
Are the caring person's
Purpose for care.

If everyone's receipt of care
Depended on payment
For past imperfections,
Or if payment for care
Must be fully extracted,
All forgiving
Would be suspended
And all possible caregiving
Fully forgotten.

41

Baggage In, Baggage Out

Cared-for persons can be difficult
For reasons
Aside from
Their reasons
For care—
  Their prior
  Problem
  Personalities.

(Which is not to say
That personality problems
Do not exacerbate
The need for care,
Or that the reason for care
Does not exaggerate
What is already there.)

Caregiver, beware.
Do not allow

103

Wisdom

That issue to be dumped
Into the caregiving lump
To be settled by you.
Meeting the need
For immediate care
Is your major issue.

(Which is not to say
That problem personalities
Of cared-for persons
Cannot change for the better—
Because of the need
Or because of the care—
They can.
Caregivers can change, too.)

42

All Things

While it is true that "things" *can* work out for good and that some, perhaps most, things *will* work out for good, many things are, at the present moment, very bad.

The quotation from Romans 8:28 in the Bible, "In all things God works for the good of those who . . . have been called according to his purpose," hardly lets us off the hook as passive pawns of fate waiting for everything to turn out well. Since God's biblically defined purpose is that we love and be loved, the activity of caregiving is obviously a major component of God's purpose.

The only way to start moving what is bad toward the good is first to admit and face it so that you know enough to elicit God's help.

105

God's will and God's plan are two different things. God's will is clear: Love God above all, and love other people as yourself (see Matthew 22:37–40). God's plan is not clear; the closest we come to having a clear view of it is in hindsight, after the fact.

God controls what we cannot control. The question becomes, What can we control? We probably can control a lot more than we realize and, on the other hand, probably a lot less.

43

Fair?

The word
Is not
In the Bible.

44

The More the Better

Wisdom is knowledge rightly applied.

You don't need a university degree to be a good caregiver, but the more you know about your cared-for one's condition, the more you know about other persons' similar experiences, and the more you know about available help, the better you will understand your needs, the more surely you will make choices, the firmer will be your decisions, the more effectively you will be your cared-for one's advocate, the greater will be your confidence in yourself, and the less likely you will have regrets.

45

Nontraditional

Who would think of me as a caregiver?

Of an adult child,
After all these years?

I? A caregiver?
I am in the slot of
Independence and freedom from
The responsibilities I had
Until my children were grown.

I am in the slot where
I am free to explore and
To be responsible
To my larger community.

I am in the slot where
I am free to be me
Before—
Oh, nagging thought—
Before I slip into the slot of being
Caregiver to the elderly

Or of being the elderly
To be cared for.

I am slipping through this slot
Too quickly.

But now
My adult child,
Who has forfeited a life and family
Established and independent of me,
Now with a shattered life, no family,
Is back home with me.

I'm involved
But not involved.

He's right
But he's wrong,
To blame
But not to blame.

And oh, God,
Where did I go wrong?
He knew better,
For he's part of me.
But how can part of me
Be an alien?

He's responsible,
But am I?

What am I to make of this?
He's home?
At his age?
Home with me?

Nontraditional

He's my child
But not a child.

I can imagine what other people think.
   He's home?
   At his age?
   Can't take care of himself?
   Needs his mother?
Is it what I think, too?

Yes.
Everyone needs someone.

He's wounded and lost
Emotionally.
He needs care,
Guidance, healing.
Why would I want him out in the world,
Abandoned by his family,
Alone?

If he needed medical care—
If he were injured or ill—
Or if he were alone
Through no fault of his own,
I would take care of him,
And other people would think
I'm wonderful to take him in.
Would we question his upbringing then?
No.

Why, now, do I look back?
I cannot care for him
With what-ifs or if-onlys,
With regrets and self-flagellations

Wisdom

Trying to undo what's done
Or put back together
What's permanently undone.

Here and now is where I live
And love;
Today I open my door
And listen,
Advise when he asks,
Express an opinion when appropriate,
Be silently steadfast, secure,
Loving
Whenever I can.
And I pray I can provide him
A base for starting over
And going forward.

Yes, I give him a bed
And share my dinner,
For he is a hurting human being
Who more than just happens to be
My son.

It's what God would do
For him
And what God
Would have me do.

46

Too Little, Too Much

Can a caregiver be uncaring?
Can a caregiver not be caring enough?
Can a caregiver be caring more than enough?
Can a caregiver be too caring?
   For the good of the cared-for person?
   For the good of the caregiver?

   Yes.

47

Respectfully Ours

God,
Infuse me with the respect
  you have for my cared-for one.

God,
Hold me to the respect
  you have for me.

God,
Enfold us all in respect
  for each other.

48

Expertise

Caregiving
Is like
Childrearing—
You know precisely
How to do it
After
It's all over.

PART Three

PEACE

Trust in the LORD, and do good . . .
and He shall give you the desires of your
heart.
Commit your way to the LORD . . .
and He shall bring it to pass. . . .
Rest in the LORD,
and wait patiently for Him.

—Psalm 37:3–7 NKJV

49

Caregiver's Prayer for Peace

God,
Turmoil and threats to the well-being of my cared-for one and me are always just around the corner. Replace my turmoil with peace and keep me free from paralyzing worry.

Thank you for implanting within me a tranquil core to which I retreat and find security and renewal and you—a peaceful place in which I can turn around, then return to my caregiving lovingly and effectively.

50

Compassion Satisfaction

To know you have been compassionate—

  have felt the feelings,
  have shared the suffering,
  have partaken of the pain,
  have been moved to mercy,
  have done as unto yourself—

Is the deepest satisfaction
Known to a caregiver.

51

Men Can, Too

Helen was lovely by any standard, and it was not difficult to see why after more than fifty years of marriage Arnie was still enthralled.

Soft-spoken but articulate, sweet but not shy, artistic but practical, small but elegant, physically beautiful—that was Helen.

Arnie, too, was small but strong, his vigor unfaltering as he advanced in age. Ever the ultimate businessman, he continued part-time consulting and same-day business trips, golfing, and guys' stuff well into his seventies. But Helen came first.

Years of asthma and steroids had taken their toll on Helen, then arthritis, then small strokes, and finally the gradual progress of senile dementia. Step by step Arnie increasingly accommodated their two-story house and his lifestyle to Helen's deteriorating medical condition, increasing pain, decreasing mobility, diminishing mental acuity, and disappearing personality. Only the latter was an obvious hardship for him.

"When someone comes to visit, you would never know she was any different than she ever was," he said. "But the minute they walk out the door she changes."

Another time: "She wheeled herself into the kitchen and said, 'Where are we?'"

And the ultimate heartbreak: "She doesn't know me."

Meticulous housekeeper, cook, medical overseer, personal attendant, night nurse sleeping on a recliner in the living room next to her hospital bed— Arnie was gladly everything to the woman who was but was not the woman he had married. Finally, he had to admit that even with home help he could no longer care for Helen and reluctantly yielded her to the nursing home.

But not completely.

He got out again for an occasional short golf game and said he was getting back his life, but three times every day he made the ten-mile round trip to the nursing home to feed Helen and oversee her care.

I once entered the main entrance of the nursing home and walked into a huddle of wheelchairs around the front desk. The bodies slumped or slouched or sleeping in them were as dull and listless as the minds they housed. But one was so stunningly beautiful I stopped short, and my mind wheeled over the incongruity. Why was such a person in such a place? Her gorgeous, perfectly coiffed silver hair literally glowed, her bearing enhanced her luxurious royal blue robe, her perfect skin and makeup dazzled. Shouldn't she be at the country club or a meeting of the symphony board?

My breath caught with sudden recognition: Helen. No wonder Arnie couldn't stay away. Helen was the living testimony that he didn't.

Eventually Arnie developed abdominal pains. The doctor knew more than Arnie. "It's not good," he said. "You're killing yourself. You have to stop worrying about Helen and quit going to that nursing home all the time."

"Oh, doctor," Arnie answered, his agony and helplessness to comply wrenching his voice, "I can't. I love her too much. I can't stay away." And he didn't.

Time passed. Helen had another stroke and died. Her years of pain and suffering were over, as were Arnie's years of easing her pain and suffering as much as was humanly possible, as much as love could make possible.

Whether or not Arnie had known what else the doctor knew he never said, but within the year following Helen's death Arnie died of colon cancer.

52

Basically It's Me

No, ma'am, she was not like this at first.
This started later.
No, there was no hint this would happen.
I guess there never is.
Or maybe we don't want to think things can happen.
Denial, I guess they call it.
Choose? No, would not have chosen this at all.
Don't guess many people would.
Sometimes, I guess, I'm still not over the shock of it.
That this happened to her. To me. To us.
Nope, not after all this time.
Well, no, it hasn't been easy.
Lots of work, sure.
And lots of things I had to learn.
I'm not an RN yet, but almost. Heh, heh.
Mostly it makes me sad.
I always feel so sorry for her.
Yup, something is always wrong.

Peace

Yes, I guess you could say I always have that
feeling.
No, I don't usually talk about it much.
Don't have time to visit with many people.
Seems more and more of my going-out time
is for taking her to the doctor and that
kind of stuff.
Getting harder to get her out, too.
And takes more time to get her ready and
settled when we get back home.

Yes, I do all the shopping.
Yup, housework. Laundry. Cooking.
Heh, heh, if you call it cooking.
I've gotten better at it, though. Microwave
helps.
Oh, my, yes. Paperwork. Gets to be more all
the time.
I think I handle it pretty well. Yes, by myself.
All that paperwork bothers a lot of people.
Hard for them.
Yes, finances, too.
Sure, terribly disappointing.
Sure, gave up a lot of my plans.
Just about all of them, I guess.
Well . . . once in a while for a short time, but
you never really get far from the situation
or get your mind completely off it.
No, not too much help. They're busy.
I don't like to bother them.
Oh, sure, they try, but you know how that
goes, heh, heh.
You can usually do it better yourself, or,
heh, heh, they're more bother than they're
worth.
Oh, sure, they mean well. I appreciate them.

Basically It's Me

Yup, basically it's me.
No, I don't look forward to much.
Hope? Umm, no, it looks pretty much
    downhill from here.
I'm not getting any younger, either, you
    know. Heh, heh.
Worry? I hope to tell you.
Two main things: money and what will
    happen.
To both of us!
To her as her condition gets worse.
What she will still go through.
If my health fails.
If I can't take care of her.
If I would die before she does.
Who would take care of her? Who would
    care the way I do?
If the money would run out. Then what?
And I'm not getting any younger, you know.

Scared. You bet! Scared to death.
Oh, I can't tell you how tired.
Overwhelmed. Yes, that's a good word for it.
I'm so sorry.
I always thought I could handle it.
I tried to be so strong.
You know, for her.
I wanted to keep her at home.
I love her.
And everyone expects you . . .
I'm ashamed . . .
I just couldn't keep up any longer.
I just caved in.
I couldn't . . .
I couldn't stop crying.
That's when they called you folks.

125

53

The Basic Me

Why, how nice of you to ask!
Yes, he's doing fine. About the same.
No, no better, no worse.
I'm fine, thank you.
Yes, I'm keeping up.
It's a big job, but I'm doing just fine.
I'm one of those people who love to take care
of people.
I wanted to be a nurse, so most of the time I
like taking care of him.
Yes, it certainly ties me down, but there are
lots of rewards.
Oh, my health is fine. I'm blessed that way.
Plenty of energy, too.
Yes, they do, but I've learned to be organized,
and I organize them, too.
I'm fortunate. I get good help.
Still, it gets hectic.
And we have our crises.
But we are given strength. Much strength.
No, not everyone understands. . . .

The time, the energy, the worry, his
   condition.
But usually I don't pay attention to that.
I just do what I have to do.
You learn to overlook a lot of things.
He's a joy to take care of, even though he
   needs a lot of care.
He has an easy personality.
He's cooperative.
He's grateful.
And he tries.
He's actually a happy person.
Yes, it breaks my heart sometimes, but I try
   not to worry too much.
I'm just happy I'm able to take care of him.
I know not everyone has it as good as we do.
But I guess the best thing is to be grateful for
   what we have.
We certainly have lots of help and
   conveniences in this day and age.
And we are so thankful we have each other.
Well, I guess you're right. I am pretty happy.
Thank you. It was nice talking to you.

54

All's Well

The morning news had been particularly distressing. Every report from a different part of the world was of people inflicting suffering and death on other people.

Nor was the weather cheerful. A wet, early-December snow had fallen but had not romantically blanketed the earth, for the walks and pavement were shiny black and wet, and the continuing snow showers only added to the sloppy mess I would have to shove off my car. I kept my lights on and drapes shut against the cold white light reflecting off the snow into my apartment.

In the afternoon I picked up some groceries and dropped them off at my mom's apartment next door. It was quiet there. I set the bag on the counter, walked through the dining room into the living room, and looked around.

The afternoon light reflected off the snow into this room also, but it was different. The drapes were palest gold, and the room was filled with muted golds and rusts and earth tones. The lighting, instead of being cold and hard, was soft and comfortable.

All's Well

The yellow-blossomed Thanksgiving mum plant, just beginning to fade, was sitting in front of the window and appeared to glow with its own inner light. The only sound was of the heat pipes ticking.

The apartment felt and looked warm.

I looked into the bedroom, and my precious, soft little bundle of a mother was in bed under her light green comforter, sleeping. She did not awaken as I watched her breathing steadily and quietly. She was eighty-five, a fragile but—for the moment—healthy little lady, my dependent. All was well with her.

I walked back through the other rooms. They were filled with my mother's presence, her glasses, her mail and books, her pens and notes, her chair, the lunch dishes she had washed and that still sat on the counter where she could reach them the next time she needed them. It was her home, just right for her.

I stood still, looking, feeling that this moment, this place, was a distillation of everything that was good in our lives: safety, warmth, comfort, beauty, nurture, love, joy, well-being—a seemingly self-contained little world, yet linked to a larger network and the outside world. I was that link. I was the caregiver who made it possible.

I remember that moment often, though in the years since, things have changed. They always do, and our memories become our major constants.

It was one of those moments in which a caregiver who has experienced increasing complexities in life has, on the other hand, learned to simplify life to its basic elements and in the simplest moments to find profound meaning, intense joy, and deep peace.

In that moment the sources of my joy came together: mother, home, security, love, God.

No negatives. Only the all's-well feeling.

55

Full Time

Only another full-time caregiver fully comprehends the phonathon syndrome and what really is put on hold.

Only another full-time caregiver fully comprehends the drop-everything syndrome and all that never again is picked up.

Only another full-time caregiver fully comprehends the forget-it syndrome and the pain of what is retained.

Only another full-time caregiver fully comprehends the endless paper-blizzard syndrome and who really is buried in the end.

Only another full-time caregiver fully comprehends my evolution to the time I suddenly stopped dead in my tracks, stamped my foot, and said, "NO! First I'm going to the bathroom."

56

Purpose: Dort

When Earl broke his hip last fall, I knew he would go to a nursing home.

In the hospital Earl was a model of uncooperativeness. Dort was in for a rough time, even with Earl in a nursing home. But the home Earl came to was his own, and his nurse was Dort.

It was bound to destroy Dort.

Dort and Earl, my across-the-street neighbors, were approaching age eighty. Earl, tall and vigorous for his age, was friendly, but he majored in negatives. He somehow thought that by voicing them strongly enough he could force them under his control.

The ever-cheerful Dort had the typical roundness of the elderly overweight and its accompanying musculoskeletal limitations. Pink sweatpants cocooned her cold legs year round, except when she went away in the car, which was seldom. Earl usually did the grocery shopping.

"I just can't do what I used to," she said. "But we know it's going to happen to all of us." By voicing the inevitable she might convince herself to accept it. I could only guess at the patience she had developed in adjusting to Earl's retirement and their move to the small house where they were almost constantly together.

Clearly Earl was the dominant one; clearly he believed it. Clearly Dort was content to let him believe it, although in her high regard for herself she remained firm.

And now this. Dort and Earl had no available extended family and counted their offspring—living their own lives on opposite ends of the county—in single digits. They attended TV church. That amounted to practically no personal support system. Did Dort know what she was getting into?

Earl was home, and winter came closer. Three vehicles came regularly: one weekly to take Dort shopping, one bearing the visiting nurse, and one the physical therapist. Now Dort instead of Earl was going out to the mailbox.

"How are *you* doing?" I asked her when we met on the street and she had reported that Earl was "coming along fine."

"I'm just great!" Did I actually detect more cheer than before?

The skies became gloomier, the weather crankier. Not Dort. "The Lord has been good to us. We have a good life!" Dort told me the next time I saw her. I heard it right. She was jubilant.

"And it isn't getting you down? You're okay yourself?" I knew the answer but still had to ask.

"Oh, yes."

Dort described a chore she had been doing in the kitchen. Earl was crowding her with his everpresent presence from his chair in the living room.

"So I said to him, 'I'm doing this, and I'm doing it my way. You just sit there and watch!'" She chuckled gleefully.

Winter closed in, and I didn't see them outside again until the first warm day in early spring. What I saw were two transformed people. Earl's walk was nearly normal. Both bubbled with joy as they told me of their gratitude to God for Earl's healing and their new appreciation of every small thing in their lives. "We are happy. God's love covers even simple people like us," Dort said.

Earl had gained a smile and shed his negatives.

Dort had shed ten pounds and ten years.

Now they both go out for groceries.

I have not seen the pink sweatpants.

57

Purpose: Earl

One morning last September, Earl was lying on his lawn off the edge of the sidewalk at the bottom of the porch steps where he had fallen and broken his hip.

One morning this April, Earl mowed his lawn.

"No one can tell me there isn't an almighty God," Earl says triumphantly. His eyes sparkle with joy, and he is nearly dancing with delight as we stop at the edge of the street to chat. Earl is eighty years old. He can scarcely tell his story fast enough.

"Nine days and nights I sat in that chair." He points over his shoulder at his house. "Without moving. I had so much pain. My wife fed me and moved the pillow under my leg and did everything for me. Nine days!

"When I lay there in the hospital, over a week, I had so much pain I couldn't eat. They gave me a pill and I threw it up. I was sick. Then they tried forcing me, and I said, 'If you leave that food in front of me I'll throw it all over.' And when they came and said, 'You have to go to physical therapy,' I said, 'Get out of my room!'"

134

Back then, Earl was a grouch.

But someone knew how to get through to him and eventually got him to physical therapy. "They told me to hang on to the walker and they put an egg under my foot. 'If you break the egg you have to go back for more surgery.' I wasn't going through all that again with all that pain, and I didn't break the egg.

"'You have to walk on your tiptoes [with the walker],' they told me. 'You have to do it if you want to walk again.'" Earl demonstrates walking on his tiptoes, now without the walker. Nearly dancing.

"So I did it. I kept doing it. And after a few weeks the doctor said, 'It's healing. Your legs are getting stronger. It's something!'"

Someone else had gotten through to Earl. "When I was in that hospital bed with so much pain, I cried out, 'Lord, take this pain from me.' And he did. It started to leave me."

"You knew God could take it from you when you asked, didn't you?" I get a word in edgewise.

"Yes, yes. Of course. In the war I was in that field, and they were falling dead all around me." He points at the remembered bodies on the ground. "I said, 'Lord, if I was born and raised to die here, so be it, but if not, if I have another purpose, I want to live!' And I was saved. I lived!"

He lived to be taken to a prisoner-of-war camp and carried its bitter baggage for fifty years.

"We don't know what's beyond this life, but it's something wonderful. Billy Graham says it's more wonderful than anything we can imagine. But now we live in the flesh; it's all we know."

I get in another word. "But it's through your body you knew the love of the Lord. Through your body you received his strength."

"Yes, yes." Earl laughs joyously.

"And through our bodies we know the love of each other. You just told me about Dort's love when she was taking care of you." Now I'm on a roll.

"Yes, yes." He laughs giddily.

"And God made your body and loves your body." I grasp his arm.

"Yes, yes." We are almost dancing together.

"Earl, I'm so happy for you. And thank you. Your telling me about your faith was a blessing to me today."

Earl no longer is a grouch. And fifty years after the war he is all purpose—praising God.

58

Feathered Comforts

The summer was one of the hottest and driest on record. The summer was the most difficult and confining on record for me and my cared-for one.

August 1 seemed to be our longest day of the summer. I had taken my cared-for one for a lengthy medical procedure in a specialist's office that morning and spent the afternoon and evening on recovery and settling down.

Later in the evening, as I carried out the trash, a birdsong coming from the tall white birch tree made me stop to look. I spied a movement high up among the leaves. The movement ensnared me.

When I returned moments later with binoculars, I sighted the same movement in the same clump of leaves. Suddenly he emerged into the full evening sunlight—a brilliant-yellow-with-black American goldfinch.

He was busily—voraciously—feeding on the tree's long tassels of fruit beads, which he somehow man-

137

aged to grab up and lay horizontally on the branch. Then, twisting himself sideways, he went to work on the row of tiny seed capsules. A second bird working farther into the tree was hidden by the leaves.

The goldfinch's brilliance, enhanced by the rays of the lowering sun and surrounding shiny green leaves, was as spectacularly beautiful as any tropical bird's in an aviary. His persistent activity was as fascinating as any circus performer's. But he was in my backyard, free to be seen, free to be he, and freeing me.

I lost track of how long I watched him. I tired before he did and realized I stood soaked in still-ninety-degree heat.

At the moment I had heard the song I became a "birder." It was a difficult time in my life, and the caregiving situation worsened over the next couple of years. But always the birds were there outside the windows, on my neighborhood walks, on short rides out into the country, on occasional visits to the nature center or the beach. I did not become— in fact, could not be nor cared to be—one of those persons who goes to the ends of the earth to seek out all possible bird species. But as I studied the bird books I identified more and more species, started a life list (goal: to see and identify all the birds of my state) and a bird-watching diary.

Later that year I wrote this in my bird diary: "I get amazing pleasure from these birds. Their existence seems to justify my time spent outside. They give me a new, broader dimension as well as intimacy with the out-of-doors and sharpen my senses, observation, mental exercise. It enters the spiritual dimension of interacting with God through God's creatures in God's creation. Now I understand the lonely people who love bird-watching—and the not-so-lonely."

I am astonished at the variety of bird species to be found in urban areas. I never tire of seeing the same kinds over and over again, for even the common birds have fascinating habits and habitats. My binoculars are always handy, and after eight years I still see new species—most near home—and learn new things. "My" birds still comfort me, pleasure me, thrill me.

We caregivers need to divert our attention to something outside the confines of our caregiving situation, if only briefly and not on schedule, something to become part of us and define us differently. My birds are an example of something uncomplicated and near at hand. Everyone's environment provides such things. Just take a look.

I have since learned that goldfinches are field birds and their favorite food is thistle seeds; they also eat other weed and grass seeds and various insects. Furthermore, in my state the white birch fruit is usually ripe and its seeds available later in autumn. Were those goldfinches eating tree seeds because the heat and drought had deprived them of their usual seeds? Had the heat and drought forced the birch fruit to mature ahead of schedule or to become palatable to those birds? Did those tiny fruit beads contain edible insects?

That August evening I heard the goldfinch's song only once. Had it signaled to its mate that the tree seemed suitable for an August nesting? Had it signaled to the other bird that food was available?

Had God inspired the bird to signal to me?

59

The Enriched One

What do I receive
From my cared-for one?

Gratitude, encouragement,
Smiles and joy

Purpose and accomplishment,
Hope and love

Significance, companionship,
Comfort and prayers

What if I received
None of the above
From my cared-for one?
Would my caring cease to be?
That would be impossible,
For even if my cared-for one
Were unable to love me,

I receive
My cared-for one—
Someone to be loved
By me.

60

The Prayer

I once had a life.

When I had everything I needed
  Then topped it with enrichment
  I was elated
  And I prayed
    a list of every blessing
    and asked why I had been singled out for
    such divine favor
    and told God my praise for every
    wonderful thing would never cease

My life changed.

When I assumed responsibilities for various
  persons
  Then disregarded a few for myself
  I was confident
  And I prayed
    a list of everything I felt able to handle
    alone
    and asked for some general sort of help
    and told God I was sure my youth and
    health would serve me well

Peace

My life changed.

When I had done everything I could
   Then tried to do more
   I was exhausted
   And I prayed
     a list of everything I was doing and still
     had to do
     and asked why I was stuck with it all
     and told God of my needs for performing
     each chore

When I had considered every angle
   Then thrust more into my mind
   I was distraught
   And I prayed
     a list of all the absurdities I must endure
     and asked if there were any scheme or
     purpose in my life
     and told God of the people and
     situations he must change

When I had absorbed every problem
   Then trusted no solution
   I was terrified
   And I prayed
     a list of everything in my life that
     threatened me
     and asked if I had been singled out for
     divine wrath
     and told God to remove every source of
     my fears

My life changed
But not for the better.

The Prayer

When I looked at the prayer
  And saw lists of specifics
  I suddenly knew that
  My prayers
    of specific requests and demands
    were nothing but formulas
    I did not trust

Life consists of cycles of specifics
That prayer encircles with the basics.

My prayer changed.

I was exhausted
  And I prayed for
    Strength

I was distraught
  And I prayed for
    Wisdom

I was terrified
  And I prayed for
    Peace

My life has changed
For the better.

I now live life's cycles of specifics
Encircled by my basic prayer for
    Strength
    Wisdom
    Peace

    and
    Praise God

61

Private Space

$\mathcal{I}$'m a little ashamed to mention this, but it's what it symbolizes that counts, I guess. It's my space on my bathroom counter that I had to give up for my cared-for person.

As spaces in the house go, it's not very significant. After all, how much time does an active adult spend at the bathroom sink? And what is that time but a stopover, a means to an end, a tiny part of the larger picture, a mere stepping-stone to the business of the day?

Compared with the kitchen, for instance, it's insignificant indeed. Food storage, preparation, and consumption require much more space and time and elaborate equipment than toothcare-skincare-haircare—one-two-three-you're-done. Take the microwave: tooth, skin, and hair stuff could all *fit* in the microwave, but what are they compared with what *happens* in it?

The center of the household is the kitchen, not one section of the bathroom counter. Yet, while both have been considerably changed—reorganized

144

and reoccupied—to accommodate our cared-for person, I'm okay about the kitchen.

So why is the bathroom counter my sore spot? Many bathrooms have no counters (for that matter, many of the world's houses have no bathrooms), but when we moved into this house, I somehow fell in love with that counter. It's a warm, light color, brightly lit, clean looking. It's big—big enough to hold everything I use, with drawers to hold it all when I'm finished so that I can quickly restore my countertop's neatness. And it's mine—my own little place. If I like or if I'm in a hurry, I can leave the mess until later. My counter just plain satisfies and delights me, my private luxury that has become my necessity.

I've given up or altered major things for my cared-for person—things to do with my job, finances, emotions, family, social time, to name a few—and many more minor. I wanted to do this, for my cared-for one is my loved one, and I think I have handled the adjustments pretty well. But certain things are best kept and used in the bathroom, so since my counter had the space for my cared-for person's things, it seemed hardly worth a second thought, only natural that . . .

I still manage to do everything I must in the bathroom, but I miss my old counter space every time I use the sink. You do understand, don't you?

62

Beginning

It's okay to scream at God.
At one time or another, most of us do.

It's part of our process
Of coming to terms
With what has become
Unbearable
For us
Or our cared-for ones—
A breakthrough,
A first step
In casting our burdens
On the Lord.

To cast our burdens
On the Lord
Does not mean
We need empty no more bedpans
Or pay no more bills
But that we relieve our hearts
Of what we cannot do
Or need not do.

Beginning

Our primal scream at God
Is a breakthrough,
A first step
In releasing to God
Control
Of what we finally know
We cannot control.

Our scream at God
Leaves us
To control
Only
What we can.

63

Conclusion

My cared-for one
Is in good hands,
God—
Yours.

64

Readiness

A dim night-light. My daughter's soft measured breathing in a peaceful sleep from which she may not awaken. I, settled into a chair next to her bed to keep vigil through the night.

We are together. We are calm. We are ready.

Readiness is a gift from God.

Like a mirror image of the beginning of her life on this earth is its end. She silently entered through a tiny channel, then flourished and grew in vibrancy. Now she has diminished, slowed, and will silently exit. And we her parents are the presence at both ends with a readiness that has embraced her life span like a pair of parentheses.

Our readiness for her birth consisted of excitement, joy, anticipation of what she would bring to us. Our readiness for her death consists of peacefully giving her up to her own eternal joy.

Without readiness we suffer. Resisting readiness, we prolong suffering. Eighteen months ago I would not have believed I would ever be ready for my daughter's death. Who could be ready for such a thing? First, with no readiness at all, came the terrible shock over the onset of her terminal illness. All of us—she and those close to her—immediately resisted readiness. We did not allow ourselves to think of her inevitable suffering and death. So began our determined fight for her life: the tests, the second opinions, the surgeries, the treatments, the trips halfway across the continent to more specialists.

Readiness was not yet ours in our anger: anger at the evil enemy inside her body; anger at the unnaturalness of a child dying before her parents and of a young mother dying who was needed by her husband and small children; anger over the unfairness of her being denied future life experiences.

Readiness was not yet ours when we expected that God, who we thought absolutely and unquestionably owed us such a favor, would simply remove this condition, this unwarranted violence against our beloved child and against our family.

Readiness was not yet ours as we became frantic over caring for her, as we attempted to relieve her of every possible bit of suffering and even tried to take it on ourselves, as we each had our own ideas of method of care and division of responsibilities to her and to each other and to her children.

Readiness was not yet ours as we grieved over our impending loss and terrible loneliness for her, over our memories of her, and over the eventual ending of the making of new memories. Greatest was our grief over the coming end to our love relationships with her.

Readiness was not yet ours as we marveled at her will to be normal, her heroic efforts to continue to squeeze happiness out of every simple thing in life, her astonishing loving acts to us that secretly broke our hearts.

But God was not going to let us decline the divine gift of readiness. Imperceptibly at first, gradually, without our thinking or trying, we began to accept the gift. We dropped our search for medical miracles, stopped fighting unwinnable battles, gave up our incredulity and regrets and anger, relieved ourselves of our health-breaking efforts to assume her care and suffering, released her to God and to other caring people, lost our fear over her husband's and children's futures without her.

Most astonishing was our new love for her. We no longer clutched her to ourselves but released her to herself to be her eternal self. I don't know how else to say it, nor can I explain how we became ever more aware of and overwhelmed by God's love for all of us.

I cannot recall when it happened, but at some point she knew we were ready, and that was the real beginning of her readiness. I think it was as though she sensed our new peace, our new strength, our new love. When we gave ourselves permission to go on without her, it was her final assurance of our complete love for her. Her dying was then, in her eyes, no longer a terrible hardship she was putting on us, no longer a burden of guilt, no longer something she inevitably had to do but from which we selfishly held her back. We allowed her to pass from the state of being terrified and wishing her dying process would never reach the point of no return and into the peaceful state of trust in God. Now she is being drawn inexorably into the irresistible being of pure eternal love, which is God. It's the last thing she told us.

I reach under the sheet and hold her hand, still warm but not for long. God has given her the gift of the ultimate readiness, and she has accepted it. Her pain stopped altogether a few days ago, she is no longer ill, her systems are gradually shutting down. She has passed the point of no return. She has no distress, only peace. She is ready to die.

I have peace. The gift of readiness is the gift of peace.

Why is my face wet? I cry over the awesomeness of this moment—its depth, its beauty, its completeness. My child and I are together, part of each other, closer than we have been since her conception. Our love of each other is more complete and purer than ever, totally embedded in and fused to God's love. I know she knows it, too.

This is a mystical moment, suspended in time, a mini-eternity.

I love you, my child—God's child. I love you, God.
Thank you, God.

65

Chronic Spouse

The hardest part of our adjustment is
Giving up
What we thought we had—
　Depended upon,
　Took for granted
　But cherished—
　　Indefinitely

The best part of our adjustment is
Accepting
What we know we have—
　Unanticipated,
　Unchosen
　But valued—
　　Enduringly

The most gratifying part of our adjustment is
Discovering
The unexpected—
　Tiny greatnesses
　In each of us,
　Between us—
　　Endlessly

66

Toenails

oenails?

Does anyone remember a time in your life
   when toenails occupied more than one and
   one-half forgettable moments?
Does anyone remember when toenails were
   of major importance in their own right?
Does anyone remember when toenails were
   objects of intricate operational campaigns?
Does anyone remember when your mother
   trimmed your toenails for you?
Does anyone remember when you began to
   trim your own toenails?

Hardly in the category of getting your driver's
   license, was it?

Would you ever have believed—before you
   became a caregiver—that toenails could
   assume a lofty position in your life?
   Someone else's toenails, that is?

Like driving a car,
Toenail trimming requires skill and practice;

Peace

Toenail trimming requires patience and cool
    heads for both parties;
Toenail trimming can be dangerous, for a
    wrong move can cause serious injury that
    results in infection or other complications;
Toenail trimming requires the right
    equipment;
Toenail trimming should be done when the
    trimmer is not tired and can see well.

But if the caregiver cannot do the trimming,
Toenail trimming requires a professional
    trimmer,
Which requires a search—usually futile—for
    a podiatrist who makes house calls
Which then requires a phone call to make an
    appointment for an office visit,
Foot washing and preparation to go out,
The trip to the office,
The wait in the waiting room,
The trimming, which is now a procedure,
The trip back home,
And paperwork: forms, payment, insurance,
    will it pay, submit the bill, etc.

Now the whole operation has cost much
    more than your first driver's license—and
    your latest. We won't even compare
    amounts of time and fun.

They never told us about this when we were
    in high school learning to live in the
    modern world as productive citizens. Now,
    did they?

Toenails?

67

Trust at Its Best

My trust in God
Is a gift from God.

When I'm at my lowest my trust becomes
    greatest;
When I'm at my worst my trust becomes
    sweetest;
When I'm most depleted my trust becomes
    purest;
For
When I'm vacant of all other reliance
My trust takes up full residence.

68

Final Chapter

Carl Olson died today.

I had known he was dying.

I was stunned when I learned he was terminally ill. We had chatted occasionally, for he and his wife, Beth, had been regular walkers past my house until autumn set in four months ago.

"He's had cancer for a year, but now he's going fast," it was reported to me in December.

In early January I was putting on my coat to leave a restaurant when I spotted Carl and Beth ready to enter the dining room. Beth came over to the rack to hang up their coats. She had aged; her face was sad and weary.

"I've heard about Carl," I said. "It's a hard time for both of you, especially Carl. But the caregiver is often overlooked, and you really need love and concern, too."

Her eyes teared as they connected with mine. "Oh, you know," she said. "You've been there, too?"

"I have." I hugged her. "I'll be praying for both of you," I said, "but especially for you."

Carl was already following the host into the dining room. I knew it was the last time I would see him.

But it was not the last time I would think of him and Beth. I must drive past their house to mine, and each time I did so during the past two months I prayed for them—especially for Beth—for strength, peace, and wisdom through God's love and presence.

Before long, different cars appeared in front of their house. Hospice. They had the best of human care. I continued to pray.

But today the cars in front of the house are of family members doing the household's tasks of the living. Today Carl has new strength, Beth her peace, and I another portion of wisdom.

And today I have gratitude for what I had been able to do for another caregiver: reach out, encourage, pray, because I "have been there" and now I am "here."

I've been a long time getting here.

Thank you, God.

69

Sequel

Carl's funeral was last week. I had not seen Beth in over two months and wished I had. But this evening I passed her house while taking my walk, and she was by her front door.

"How are you doing?" I asked as I approached the porch. We both ignored the cliché, and I walked up the steps.

"Oh," she said, "I want you to know your hug has been such a help to me."

"Really? And I've wanted you to know I prayed for you every time I drove past your house."

"I knew people were praying for us," she replied. "But your hug was just what I needed that day. I've told people about it. I told all my kids. It was a bad day. We had just been to the doctor. Sometimes you get what you need in unexpected places."

"That's true," I said. "Carl was already walking into the dining room. I knew it was the last time I would see him."

"Really?"

"Yes, but I knew you had your needs—encouragement and prayers."

"Sometimes the Lord moves us to do certain things," she said.

"That's what happened. And people who have been caregivers understand other caregivers. I've prayed for peace and strength and wisdom for you."

"We had forty-eight years together," Beth told me. "We were close. It was a good marriage."

"It's wonderful to have that," I replied, "but the separation is still awful. There's no comfort for that. Your comfort is elsewhere."

"We have hope. Carl is well now," she said serenely but firmly.

Beth talked briefly of her adjustments and future plans. And we talked about prayer. I said I would continue to pray for her and that I believe it is important to tell people I am praying for them. It's important to the effectiveness of the prayer and to the people for whom I pray.

It's part of my way of passing on comfort and encouragement.

But as I walked back home I was awash in the feeling that I had received comfort and encouragement from Beth.

We are the caregivers.
We are a multitude.

Afterword

Strength comes with hope.

Wisdom begins with love.

Peace grows with faith.